DISTORTED

You deserve your intended life

2nd EDITION

BY
MARLYN ROJAS

Distorted
You Deserve Your Intended Life
2nd Edition

©2021, 2025 Marlyn Rojas

All rights reserved solely by the author. The author guarantees all contents are original and do not infringe upon the legal rights of any other person or work. No part of this book may be reproduced, stored in a retrieval system, or transmitted in any form or by any means without expressed written permission of the author. Scripture taken from the New King James Version®. Copyright © 1982 by Thomas Nelson. Used by permission. All rights reserved.

Printed in the United States of America ISBN -13: 978-1-7343346-7-8

Radiant Publishing

Typeset by: Michelle Cline

FOREWORD

Knowing Marlyn in the way that I know her, I feel privileged to be able to tell you about this book, that God, for her history and experiences has allowed her to write. I believe with all my heart that God allowed her to do it having in mind the youth, women, and men that are going to be transformed through the pages of this work. She speaks openly so that every reader understands what a rampant life is, without God, without hope and how at a time when she decides to change the course of her life, through drawing near God, she manages to turn her life 180°. I motivate you to read this work and I assure you that if you take the example of her life and decide to give yourself a chance, through the knowledge of God and an approach to Him, your Life can also be transformed. I know that many will be transformed, edified, and blessed. This book will unleash the power to overcome.

Pastor David Serrano- (RIP 1950-2021)

ACKNOWLEDGEMENTS

I am so honored to serve a personable God that allowed me to have access to Him.

I dedicate this 2nd Edition of my book to Him first and above all, as He guided me precisely through each step of the way. Thank you, Father!

Secondly my family, in which maybe we never saw any of us writing a book- ever! but today I say I am standing today and representing us all through this book. Thank you for believing in me! Love you all!

Third, to my dear mentor and pastor until 2021, Rev. David Serrano, who has helped me to be molded into the woman that God called me to be. Thank you for being a man of integrity.

Lastly, to all the friends and mentors chosen by God, who have supported me from day to day, and to my future children–Your momma's first book is here!

CONTENTS

FOREWORD iii
ACKNOWLEDGEMENTS v
INTRODUCTION ix
I'VE BEEN THERE TOO 1
I WAS IN DENIAL! 5
YOU MUST DETOX, WHAT YOU
    BELIEVED TO BE RIGHT! 9
I WAS OPEN AND WISE ENOUGH TO MAKE THE BOLD
    DECISION OF UNDERSTANDING "THE SOUL" 13
BE OPEN TO STARTING A PRAYER LIFE, IN A BOLD
    RADICAL WAY 17
REVELATIONS STRAIGHT FROM ABOVE! 21
STUDY FEMINISM 27
DECLARE AND KNOW THE PROMISES OF GOD OVER
    YOUR LIFE 33
CONTENTMENT IN ALL SEASONS 37
IT'S ALL ABOUT THE CALLING AND PURPOSE 43
YOUR INTENDED LIFE WORKBOOK 47

INTRODUCTION

The Marlyn you're seeing now is nowhere near the Marlyn from years ago. Now I'm in awe when anyone asks for advice from different walks of life. I remember five years ago (2015) when I finally realized how many things I have been holding on to and tied to from my childhood and my adolescent years that I had to release. I also didn't realize how much fault I had in my toxic relationships, besides my partner. I was as guilty as them and I went into tears as I realized this. I wept for hours while reviving the pain of both pushing away good men and good friendships in my life because I didn't value them nor saw a need for them. I had an entire life carrying burdens because I wanted to be and act like a man and his functions in every single way without noticing; from any duties at home to anything done outside whether, at school, college, work, or hanging out, and simultaneously wanted to still "act" and remain being known as a great woman- the Ms. Independent one. All of this opened up, as people say a "CAN OF WORMS," which I call:

> **"A CAN OF EMOTIONS THAT NEED HEALING"**

I never realized how many relationships I was affecting, the anxieties and sporadic depression I was fighting, the cycle of a toxic relationship I was confronting the wrong perspectives in many areas in my life I was facing including any future relationship, marriage, and children. That one-day my life changed forever and I've never been the same!

Everything I am about to share in the next few short-inspiring- yet practical- chapters is to boldly help you get to the root of the problems that **WOMEN** are silently battling, in denial or simply are not aware of; therefore is affecting every aspect of their life. If it's been affecting your identity, singleness, dating/ courtship, engagement, marriage, motherhood, interpersonal relationships with your family- including children, separation, and a divorced season; or if you are a **MAN** trying to understand it: then this book is for you! Allow me to serve your needs by sharing the journey, secrets, and practical things to be RENEWED and get you to the best intended life God made for you! So let me have a personal conversation here with you. I wish I had someone to give me a blueprint like this one to follow step by step but I did not. I went through an entire two year season from Aug 2014 to Sept 2016 -Alone- just to now birth a book like this one to help women (or men) into boldly accelerating them back to the originally designed life that was meant for them. These two years embarked on a lot of details, journeys, and revelations my friend, including resigning from being an NYPD Police Officer. Which, I had to dedicate its own book to that experience- to help women, or any man to help their partner, understand deeper revelations given to me straight from God. In this book, I will try mentioning the core process, within those two years that I had to go through to get you back to the original plan meant for you!

CHAPTER 1
I'VE BEEN THERE TOO

Just like in simple math the common denominator was I and is always ME in everything good or bad that it's happening or has happened in my life! So change needed to start with ME, to be able to impact or be the difference in everything that was and maybe going wrong or right at the time. Therefore, the common denominator is you and change must start with you!

That may sound cliché, but guess what? It's where I need you to start so that I can serve you with excellence and you will see the fruits over your life as transformational after reading this book. Just like me, people will notice the change in you as well.

Now, I knew I had such a need for a breakthrough that I did not want to go back to the old me. So, my friend, you must be very serious about a true genuine change because when you are, your life would not be the same! That exceptional change is what I was waiting for, what I longed for and didn't want to let more time pass me by and feeling like a failure in many areas of my life. As a human I understood relationships are important—no one is in this world on their own, and I wanted all relationships across the board to be healthy and radical, not just normal according to society standards. I knew that the impossible could happen through me! I now know it's all because of God that the possibilities live in me.

TOO SIMPLE TO BE EFFECTIVE.

When I realized my childhood upbringing was infiltrating my ways as an adult that called my attention. I literally did a list with two columns on plain paper. The first column will say:

All the bad moments or situations I can recall from my childhood, a line down the middle to split the page, and the column across will say *"what are the negative impacts to my character"* nowadays as an adult. This might definitely sound too simple to be effective. Well, you can sit there and criticize it, or you can sit there and actually try it. Only in trying it yourself, you would identify its effectiveness. What these columns help me see would be the same for you! You would be able to see *the roots of every problem or situation you were facing at the moment of that situation*, or that you are facing right now! And I'll share the most impactful breaking point in my life- from my past- that I wrote in my "BAD moments side of the column, and i quote: "*at the age of 12 years old my dad cheated on my mother over and over again- mom forgave him so many times- but finally, she decided to leave dad for good.*" When I began to analyze the negative impact this situation had on my character as an adult, as I wrote this list, I realized something unintentionally my mother had done. Till now I live under this following revelation from that moment, which brought me to tears. My mother had inculcated in my sister and I, from a root of an emotion of pain and hurt, to grow up and learn to be Ms. Independent in all ways possible, because in reality "we didn't need a man to do anything for us" and that when marriage comes it comes, but by then you'll know how to do it all. (I am only expressing in words the emotion behind what was instilled in us).

Now, to even realize that this was a negative impact on my character and not a praiseworthy one, was shocking. Now, remember that mom's heart, though wounded, was teaching her daughters what she thought to be best so that her daughters never suffer in the future in the same way, and daddy as a father was and is exemplary. I now know that it was God that revealed this to me and placed it in my heart. All of a sudden I was able to realize again that if ALL my past relationships have gone bad or toxic in any way or another, *the common denominator was ME*, therefore, I had to realize that there are many areas in my life, in the inner me that I need to give a chance to accept change.

> *the common denominator was ME*

No one loses anything by trying. The worst thing that can happen, if it didn't work, I can always return to the old me. I am certain that won't happen, nor would it cross your mind after you read this short helpful book.

On the other hand, I still chose to do a column of all that I believed were good moments or situations in my childhood, keyword "believed," and likewise, on the other column their consequences/impact on my character as an adult. This helped me to see that some of my upbringing allowed me to build a few of my strengths that I could execute today, and likewise some I believed were good still brought a negative impact to my character at the moment. So, this brought me to the *second simple task that you might say*: is too simple to be effective, but again I did this too, and it can change your life. *I went ahead and wrote out a list of all that I believe to be my weaknesses and another column of strengths*, In doing so I was able to analyze each of them, one by one, and see how some of our *weaknesses* are hidden strengths. The process of analyzing it, besides bringing it to God in prayer (having a talk with God, but I'll share about that later) I went through each word/phrase and would try to dig, and search deeper, and think in what way this one thing can be a weakness or a strength in my life, and to serve what purpose in my life or someone's life?

This led me to the third simple task I did: seeing if my current *strengths* will clarify my purpose and destiny in my life. To me, it cleared up much confusion, and answered many questions and if you take your time and do this it would definitely help you get much closer to your calling, purpose, and destiny in your life. Especially being led by a Certified Life Coach/Mentor as myself / or a Leader you may trust.

REMEMBER THIS:

"YOU ARE NOT HERE ON EARTH JUST TO EXIST!

There's a PLAN BEYOND your situations, sickness, circumstances, and worries."

CHAPTER 2
I WAS IN DENIAL!

I was determined to find change and a healthy lifestyle in my future, destiny, purpose, and overall all my relationships. I remembered that all successful people have one thing in common, at least 99% of the time, they read. They have a consistent habit of reading, feeding their brains. Now, my understanding is that many times the books they are reading are self-help books, with bible principles, *that remove God from them*; I realized the importance of reading the bible because it's the actual source where many of these "great" self-help books come from. Also, I kept reading other books, mainly Christian ones, to help me understand some of the biblical principles I may have questions about. I do recommend everyone to also read: **"Ordering My Private World" by Gordon McDonald, "Calm My Anxious Heart" by Linda**

"Ordering My Private World" by Gordon McDonald, "Calm My Anxious Heart" by Linda Dillow, and "Biblical Femininity" by Christie Cole. Men and women should read these.

Dillow, and "Biblical Femininity" by Christie Cole. Men and women should read these. What I realized as a woman of Faith, that the bible is God's voice, and now I would not stop reading the real source from all these other "master books" out there. (Many years ago, in network marketing, I remember they urged us to read self-help books; which also meant they knew and understood the importance of feeding your mind).

> **"The mind has to be FED to cause CHANGE."**

From there on this became a very important task for me, and a hard one, because I, like many people, did not like to read. Knowing that a habit takes 21 days to build, I decided to read my bible at least 5-10 min daily, morning and night, and a secondary Christian book (especially the ones I've mentioned above) at least for 10 min as well, after reading the bible. This I consistently did, without hiccups, for 21 days straight, and it became a habit, and it went on into 6 months and into my lifestyle. What occurred after this, while also asking God in prayer to put the love for reading back inside of me, is that I literally began to love to read once again, so much that nowadays I read about 2-3 books a month with the little spare time I have, which is not a lot, but I make sure I dedicate time to reading and so can you! This also allowed me to experience the power of prayer even with the smallest things and details before the Lord. Also, I came to see the power of the bible and its principles.

After you are able to reach these basic steps, something massive begins to happen inside of you, your love for God grows which in essence you begin loving yourself again since He created us. Only the creator of something can begin to describe what the product is and all its functions. I began to know me and who I was through the word of God- and so will you!

I began reading the four gospels in the New Testament of the bible; and would underline every single characteristic of JESUS that I would come across, and then almost simultaneously began reading Psalms and Proverbs as part of my morning prayer routines, then Romans, and 1 & 2 Corinthians to study later on the day. Again I was doing this for me, and I was determined to uncover the truth behind living a life of fulfillment through knowing my original plan that many don't talk about.

CHAPTER 3

YOU MUST DETOX, WHAT YOU BELIEVED TO BE RIGHT!

We as humans have no idea of how much things were planted and inculcated in our lives from our childhood. We tend to not go back and realize how many wrong things we have learned from the past are affecting us now. All that "wrong" we bring and drag it forward into our lives, our marriage, our children, and all our relationships in general. I'll tell you the secret; you need to literally DETOX! Unlearn the learned things, get cleansed from what you believe is right and get rid of some of it, if not all of it. When it's pertaining to this distorted life that you're living in, again I am assuming you know how toxic relationships and lack of understanding your design is a current issue or an area that needs improvement. Maybe you want to learn more of it and find a solution to the root of the problem that is not letting you live the life you deserve.

LISTED ARE THE STEPS I TOOK TO DETOX.

A. I am very visual, so I went back to that LIST of the negative and positive impacts and I literally prayed to God to help me be open in the areas I thought I was correct and to open my eyes to see and be enlightened when there was room for improvement.

B. I made the decision to let it all go when it pertains to an area that I acknowledge I needed help in, understanding me, who I was, and the things I've learned.

C. Throughout my daily walk whenever I spoke to anyone, women or men, I was carefully thinking of my thought process, intentionally seeing from which root it is coming out of.

For example: if a man held the door, and I'm ready to grab it from their hand and say, "No thank you I got it". I would stop myself and simply think and say in my mind "I want to answer this way but I would do the opposite. Therefore my literal answer will be "Oh, thank you very much sir" as I pass the door the man would be holding open. You must start choosing to purposefully and intentionally do the opposite of certain things, to deceive my brain, my habits, and my old ways, which would open room to get my brain ready for new needed information and not be conformed to the old ways. This is not easy at all but doable!

> **"YOU MUST BE INTENTIONAL!"**

D. I never let go of those books I mentioned before because they dealt with detoxing the inner me. Any given moment

I needed a pick me up, or part of my daily self-examination, I went back to those books and to my underlined or highlighted points that ministered to my heart.

CHAPTER 4

I WAS OPEN AND WISE ENOUGH TO MAKE THE BOLD DECISION OF UNDERSTANDING "THE SOUL"

I followed and studied very closely preachers that truly understood the soul, and my all-time favorite at the moment and highly esteemed till this day, may he rest in peace, and is Dr. Myles Monroe. I would never forget the way one of his examples to understand the soul was engraved so deeply in my mind, that my life was never the same. He explained it with three humans from the congregation. At the time I watched this on a platform called YouTube. The example he used went this way: one individual represented the BODY, another individual was standing in the middle as the representation of the SOUL, and the third was the SPIRIT (in this case the HOLY SPIRIT, which means when a person allows God to come into their heart by accepting the Lord Jesus Christ as their Savior and God's Spirit comes to live in the person so now the person has his HUMAN SPIRIT NOW COMBINED WITH GOD's SPIRIT)

So he explained how all of our senses bring Information to the BODY (the first individual standing)... and the BODY transfers it to the SOUL (the person that was in the middle), but he paused to explain that the SOUL is the MIND, WILL, and EMOTION (also the conscious and sub- conscious), and then the SOUL is supposed to take the information received to the SPIRIT (the third individual) to see if it's pleasing to God, to seek guidance from our CREATOR through His

Spirit. Now that's the one we choose to either ignore or listen to. Why? Because we ALL POSSESS THE WILL (inside the soul). We decide if we heed or not to the council that the

SPIRIT IS TELLING US, which is STRAIGHT FROM THE BIBLE, the Word of God. And many times our WILL takes over and just turns and ignores the SPIRIT (the third indi- vidual) and just tells the body to act this way or that way based on the emotions and to ignore what the SPIRIT is saying. In the same way, the part of the SOUL- the mind- which receives the information from the five senses passes that information to our conscious and subconscious, therefore you must reject it or accept it; because one or the other will be manifested, YOU will act on it.

Let me try a visual of the scenario below:

At this point, I went on to understand more once he explained that the devil WORKS WITHIN AND THROUGH AIRWAVES (MUSIC, SHOWS, MOVIES, CONVERSATIONS, etc). The Devil, the enemy, who is out to kill, steal, and destroy, wants to get to your subconscious, which is in our mind, which is in our soul, so that the will can decide, then the body may act on it (follow through with wrong decisions), and he does it through everything your five senses connect to.

If this didn't shake you, it shook me! At this point, I chose to make drastic decisions in my life from here on and it began exactly with that: what music I'm listening to, is it feeding my soul non-sense or making me more susceptible to hearing God's word and voice. I didn't used to read much, but what was I reading? I knew by reading the helpful books I mentioned before, I was now feeding my soul right. Also, I began to think about who I'm constantly surrounded by, and any impact on me of listening to their words and conversations? And lastly, what am I watching? And these are only to name a few of the drastic changes to consider. You must ask and answer these questions to yourself.

I will share an impactful drastic decision for me; it was listening to worldly music. I cut it completely out of my life, especially Salsa and Bachata (Hispanic traditional music)... you may ask why or call me radical. Let me explain! I realized right away the minute I tried listening to it again, that it would remind me of any ex-boyfriend right away, or it would put me in a sullen gloomy mood, or sadness would come over me. It was clear this is not healthy for someone trying to change his or her ways. So never again was I willingly putting this type of music in my vehicle, at home, or at work by choice. I started playing anything that would feed my soul correctly and that was Gospel music for me. You need to realize what's good for your soul. (Some music may not necessarily speak a ton of curses in the lyrics so you might assume it is not bad to listen to, but if it's not lifting your spirit then it might still not be beneficial for you.) Key biblical life principle: **"Everything is permissible in life, but not everything is beneficial."**

"Everything is permissible in life, but not everything is beneficial."

As you can see, understanding the soul took me to a deeper detoxing that I had no idea it would lead me to.

CHAPTER 5

BE OPEN TO STARTING A PRAYER LIFE, IN A BOLD RADICAL WAY

In a bold radical way, it means when you skip hanging out to be in a room sitting still, hearing God's voice (and God may speak differently to every person). I personally had to go into what I call "THE CAVE TIME." I remember this was a point in my life where I wanted radical changes, in my Faith, in my walk, in my decisions, in my everything and I thought wanting more or getting busy while doing more was the solution, and in reality, it was backward.

> **"To have more in God you must learn to do less for a season"**

I did not realize God was putting me in a CAVE TIME to allow me to be stripped away from everything. God spoke to me through prayer straight to my spirit, and through the bible twice, where He asked me to resign my current job at the time as a Police Officer for the New York State Police Department. (I share direct personal encounters and experiences that GOD showed me while in the department to share with women just like you -or your partner or women you know- and be free from further inner battles that they are dealing with; in the dedicated (next)book: STRIPPING AWAY THE VEST. At the time I only had about 10 months in the department when the decision to leave the department began to marinate in my heart.

> "But when GOD requires a drastic change from you, HE will back you up and help you finalize that decision."

I noticed that same week I began to feel as if my love for the job was decreasing, not wanting to go into work the same way I did a few days prior. I did not understand until I later understood that it was GOD preparing my heart for the transition I was about to experience once I left the job about three months later. As the Good FATHER that HE is, He takes care of His children. Please note, I was already in a consistent prayer life. Notice, I said consistent, not ultimate prayer warrior, just consistent at this point which I built by pushing myself to do everything mentioned in the prior chapters).

Three months after "preparing my heart for the transition", God spoke to me two more times and it was clear as day that He said to get out and resign. He gave me two dreams back to back where God said in Spanish, "I place you in a **cave** like Elijah, so that you begin to **know me** on a new level" and secondly He spoke to me through His Word with two different bible verses that pierced my heart. I resigned January 29, 2016. My "cave time" within these two years of "stripping away the vest" began to get even deeper. God had to uproot some hard cemented things and He was going to use my free time the same way He will use your devoted time solely for this purpose! **Uproot!**

I began studying the Word more, fasting (refraining from food and water for a few hours to disconnect from the world and connect more with God), journaling daily to have records of my process understanding that one day I would see the fruits of this moment–as I once heard from Kim Walker. But journaling was also the process of venting, and not necessarily to people. Little did I know my journals were writing many parts of my books. Also, writing down my prayers and their fulfillments in their due season. I began watching more preaching's on the platform called YouTube, listening to various worship music all day. My routines on church days were, wake up early, pray, read the bible, read my Christian books, journaling etc., but skipping many invitations just to stay home, most of the time in my room focused (since I lived with other family members, and though I shared rooms, once they were out of it, I would lock myself in with their permission). Then, if there was a church service, I would head to church and come right back straight home. Understanding this was needed since I was known to always be out, spending time with friends, and not knowing how to be home spending my time wisely for my personal growth.

> **I know it might sound radical, BUT I wanted radical change.**

Moreover, God told me not only to leave the job of NYPD, but to back down from Ministries–this was still Him as a Good Father taking care of my Spiritual Life, and making sure I did not get burned out in serving the church or many areas a little too much. He knew a break was needed before He let me back in at His time.

I did not step down from ministry or anything I did, expecting to get right back at it, all the contrary, I wanted to enjoy the process fully and let GOD be GOD. This is when I began to have deeper revelations that surpassed my understanding, but until today help me move forward. One of them was:

> **"Contentment is tied together with enjoying your new season and in this season appreciate all that you have and do not have. I came to an internal state at heart where I did not want anything else but Christ."**

CHAPTER 6

REVELATIONS STRAIGHT FROM ABOVE!

This was huge for me, and STILL IS! I remember pushing myself beyond my norm, and sitting in a dark room to simply talk to God, Oh yes, you read correctly- a DARK ROOM. I realized many of us are afraid of just sitting and being still, but even more of being in a dark place, no distractions, lights off, no music, where all you hear is your breathing and your words. I understood this was furthermore part of my internal detox and that I truly wanted to learn to be still and know he is God. To "know" something/someone means there's an action involved, therefore:

1. Revelation was that: *There is a Movement In His STILLNESS.* When being still in His presence you learn to hear His voice. I began to feel the Spirit of God reveal many things internally. I remember a time of just weeping, at the moment God allowed me to see a flashback "movie" of my life and my past and the way my past had affected who I was today. That there were roots I did not want to accept, because I lived in denial as if certain

actions and characteristics were "OK." and that is when the second Revelation came.

2. It is ABSOLUTELY NOT BIBLICAL to be Ms. Independent and if I didn't put a genuine change to this there was no reason for God to take me into any other new levels in Him, because I would be stepping down into any men in my life and not submitting to authority, which is rebellion. This is always hard to GRASP! Let me try to simplify it. The more I began to learn to depend on God alone and honor the essence of God being a gentleman, a provider, a loving God; I would be able to honor the same exact qualities in a man–that already possess such designs. Learning to DEPEND on Him.

3. I wept so hard when I realized how many men in my past I had probably hurt. God was not bringing this to the surface to condemn me, but to heal me, and to allow me to see the value in releasing myself from such false doctrine. Which one? The one where we accept the world and its society to instill in us that it is biblical to not honor the men in our lives.

> "It is not ok to now claim to be a woman of GOD and act exactly the same way the world wants women to be out in the world- AGAINST OR STEPPING on MEN- THERE IS STRENGTH when you learn the established order by GOD from God's Original PLAN from the beginning."

These were three main revelations that led me to a hunger of SEEKING HIS WORD MORE, searching more, studying more, which is what I did next, but before I move on to the next let me just share the OTHER REVELATIONS THAT CAME OUT FROM THESE "STILL-MOMENTS," which led to intimacy like never before with my GOD.

Listed in no specific order, these are more of my revelations:

- He is truly my Father, no matter whatever my earthly fathers had or haven't done

- There were chains broken from my generational curses passed down by family that I had no idea existed, but I prayed them OFF ME (example: alcoholism, lottery bondage, believing in Saints and Santeria)

- Be child-like, we do not know it all, and is ok to accept that you are still learning

- Overall put on Love

- God has OPENED my eyes (Spiritually speaking we are often blinded)

- True Submission and Dependency in Christ is STRENGTH

- Learned how to tune out the noise of my surroundings

- Learned Contentment in ALL seasons of life and NOT TO COMPLAIN

- Learned that in moments of feeling the Lowest is where God Loves to Glorify Himself

- Be Faithful even with your thoughts

- A man chooses His wife, we do not force, we do not chase

- Learned to never Give up, Persevere

- The Lord Bets on you when afflictions come your way   that you will withstand

- You've learned that when you obey against all odds, you see God's hands over your life

- Learned what it means to be one body in Christ- united!

- You now know that you know that God and only God are in CONTROL in His Sovereign and perfect will!

- Learned to be a prayer warrior

- Learned to LET GO and LET GOD- to surrender it all

- The deeper the foundation, the higher the sky-scrapers, the arrow must go back 1st before going forward

- You know that in your intimacy He allowed you to see DEEP hidden things to become more like Him

- You do not follow man-made rules! You are doing things backward/contrary with PURPOSE! (Obeying God's way)

- Remember at all times that FIRE refines you!

- God will test individuals depending on their calling

- Remember that you belong to God first- ABOVE ALL, YOUR FIRST LOVE and YOUR HEART IS IN HIS HANDS, Safe Haven!

- At TIMES pounder things in your heart, without having to always share them with others

- He takes care of you and your blessings, while you take care of His matters, Kingdom matters, seeking Him first

- Praying from Victory stand, you manifest the Spiritual to the Natural

- When I am weak, He is Strong

- Be Faithful with things that belong to others, Give the very best of you in ALL you do

- In deep waters, the risky waters, it's a divine set-up for you to know Him deeper, personally, and see His Glory

- Our Promises are within our reach, not in our hands- Move in prayer! –P. Shirer

- Look at others as a father looking at a child- so the way GOD LOOKS AT THEM

- Learned who God IS, and His Essence, His Character- which means I was made to His image and Likeness

KEY POINT: The REVELATIONS above were given to me during different times of prayer, reading, just sitting still, dreams, visions, and more. Therefore, I literally had a loose-leaf taped to my wall by my bedside with a pen nearby and every single time a new revelation was shown, I would write them down. I would read my entire list day and night, until about one and a half years later when my character truly began to look a bit more like the Jesus who rescued me and I highly recommend for you to do the same.

CHAPTER 7

STUDY FEMINISM

"Are the biblical patterns and battles faced in such times, the same ones we face today?"

The answer to that question is yes. See I came to understand that when the enemy attacks us one way, and it works, he will try to continue using that same tactic because it worked the first, second, or third time around. In the same way from the beginning the devil saw women, (Eve being the symbolic person for all women in design and calling), was deceived using one tactic and strategy and it worked. He keeps using the same tactic even today against all of us.

I'll recap the key points of feminism that helped me and opened up my eyes and bring in the word in between these points that helped me have a clearer understanding.

The bread and butter of feminism are what you need to remember. We are not being unappreciative of the great accomplishments that women are able to now have, such as voting, being able to work, going to colleges for a degree and more. But I want to show you how something that is meant for good, just like many good things out in the world with good intentions, the enemy tries to distort it and encourages us humans to abuse its purpose.

"When you don't know the purpose of something it's inevitable to not abuse it" -Myles Munroe

The truth is that "for over 50 years, **The Feminist movement, wants women to act like men, no different than God disliking men acting like women**" and this was a phrase I read in a documentary years ago that always stood with me.

"*The Feminist movement, wants women to act like men, no different than God disliking men acting like women*"

- Feminism is taking the God-given design and taking it to the extremes of abusing it and using it against men, the same men that you long for.

- Feminism goes against many biblical principles such as, truly being counterpart strength to your mate- not a competition but cooperation- we don't always have to be right.

- Women guard your heart above all things. We are NOT physically stronger, but we can be an emotionally stronger support to anyone, especially men.

- Face off fear so that your children hear His Promises- unlimited. Confident women face their fears and in that, you sometimes find your strength. God is NOT interested in the areas where you are strong and He is weak.

- We are costumed made for His glory!

- Confident women know how to handle their sword (THE WORD); to us as daughters–we need to transfer HONOR, GLORY, LEGACY, and TITLE with God's word usage

- We are the glory of men! That should be all men. (The single woman needs to be the glory of the men in their lives, ex: their brother, their pastor, and their mentor)

- What is GLORY? That which inspires awe, wonder, or splendor; amazing!

- Women draw their husband near anything-INFLUENCE. (We have the gift of healthy influence), unless we abuse this and build an unhealthy use for it.

- Confident women guard the man's heart (Proverbs 31:11) "The heart of her husband safely trusts her, so he will have no lack of gain. If we focus on acting and being like men, we truly are not guarding our heart, nor theirs. We are allowing a cracked door to be deceived in different matters emotionally, romantically, and Spiritually.

- Build your marriage, your relationship, pointing out each other's strengths.

- To also battle the "feminist mindset" I read and study: *Biblical Femininity* on a deeper scale the second time around and underlining and praying on topics I realized I needed help with.

Men's greatest sin, according to Genesis, right before the fall of men, is passivity. Adam could've told Eve the instructions he got from the Lord, Adam was there, but stepped back, let passivity kick in. Hence, we have seen throughout the years and until today that many men find it hard to stand up into their masculine role and function.

Women's greatest sin, according to Genesis, is autonomous. The women get deceived by beginning to visualize the fruit as good fruit, and I don't have to ask Adam if it's right, I visualize it, I will be like God, therefore I will eat, it's my decision- autonomous, doesn't it sound a lot like feminism? We have to be extra careful with the way the devil gets into our homes, our minds, our lives because he knows it worked in the beginning, so why not now? Short testimony, while I was still a police officer, which truly allowed me to break a stronghold in my life with this autonomous attitude. It was on Thanksgiving day of 2015. I remember joining a friend and her family, including her brother, whom at the time I was getting to know for possible dating reasons. I remember after having dinner we all began singing unto the Lord, praying for one another. At a given moment one of my friends asked me to pray for his feet, symbolizing his journey and where God will take him. I remember feeling a bit awkward, or a bit shameful, thinking to myself " I'm about to bow down to the feet of a man," -stay with me- yes it was symbolic, but here was the Ms. Independent in me, the many thoughts the devil places in our minds, the on denial woman not accepting a problem of lack of authority established by God- and as I went to the floor and grabbed his two feet and began to pray, something began to happen! I wept, and wept, and wept! I felt strongholds being loose! I felt a Spiritual release which till today it's still hard to explain. I remember hearing the same friend that asked me to pray, from afar, saying "guys she's not just praying, at this point, she is having her own inner breakthrough" and that's exactly what was happening internally. God was releasing me from the autonomous spirit stronghold. It is real and active! As a woman, we have to intentionally be aware of this major sin.

Let me share a recap with you on our MEN AND WOMEN DESIGNS is the following:

MEN:

Priority: Foundation of the human family; Position: Continually in God's Presence;

Assignment: Visionary, Leader, Teacher, Cultivator, Provider, Protector, (later after marriage: Financial/ Support/emotional/ and intellectual Support.

Needs a COMPANION: 3 major needs to be fulfilled: SEX,

RESPECT, RECREATIONAL COMPANIONSHIP

WOMEN:

Primary Purpose: receive Love from the male, just as God's Purpose for creating the Spirit -man was to have a relationship of love with mankind (GEN 1:28)

Secondary Purpose: Dominion over the earth

Women are: Enhancers, companions (counterpart strength, corresponding to men and others), Good, Shares, Encourages, a Reflector, an incubator.

Needs: LOVE, CONVERSATION, AFFECTION

Important key things I instilled in my mind from Myles Munroe's teachings and remembering that:

MEN & WOMEN cannot function in the Harmony and effectiveness outside God's plan

SATAN IS AFRAID of the POWER of a MAN and WOMAN united in God's Presence

CHAPTER 8

DECLARE AND KNOW THE PROMISES OF GOD OVER YOUR LIFE

You might think exactly what I thought at the moment, "everyone is always talking about the promises of God but no one is really saying how do I even begin to start believing them?"

I literally thought the same. Or even "How do I get to know them?"

I began my search, so you need to start your search, no one but you must do it. The journey of uncovering His promises was exactly the process that allowed me to fall in love with the amazing God of the heavens.

The yearning, the longing, to seek and read His word more than ever was growing each and every day while I was thinking I'm just searching for promises. I've come to learn that when any book gives you just a list of many promises you do not internalize them the same way! I cannot do that disservice to you; hence the reason you or someone you know doesn't do well with daily devotionals at times. There's nothing wrong with them, but they are based on someone else's experience, shoot to have your own experience so that you are the one that can testify of a transformed life one day! Now, believe it or not, this needs to start with you pushing yourself to read THE BIBLE in two ways: from the beginning, Genesis, Exodus, especially and simultaneously reading Psalms and Proverbs. As you read, be observant of the promises of the Lord that jump out of the page, and write them down! Do not rely on your memory, put paper where you can see it by your bedside.

Something else I did with these promises, I took it further! I created my own *health aid kit*. "An emergency kit for dyer moments, or any day that I need to be reminded of the change God has done over my life, and His promises for me." I literally took index cards, construction color papers, and grabbed markers and became even more creative. I wrote some of my promises down, and also any favorite bible verses that were uplifting. Remember, this is a box to uplift you in those tough days. Then I searched for a beautiful box that defined me, but instead, I chose one that defined the area where God is dealing with me. Because God had been dealing with my biblical femininity, I chose to use a poke-dot colorful mini box, 5x5x5 to be my emergency box (I highly recommend for you to choose one where God is dealing with you, or if you start with one, you can upgrade to the other down your journey). If by now you have journal-in, or simply remember ANY word from God that He has given you from your childhood till this moment, this is the time to also write them down on one of these papers and place them in the box.

Also, include any items that define the beautiful personality that you have and even items that define new changes in you. For example, I put a tiny ballerina because God gave me the dancing talent, and heart that rejoices and dances like David in the bible. I also added a small wooden piece that said "Prayer Warrior" because I saw how in my cave time God was making me a prayer warrior. Find yours.

Lastly, I began to make sure I have a set place for me to study and seek the Lord. In this place, I always added verses, and visual things, that when I see it it encourages me to seek God. In my case, I made sure my desk had my bibles right on top, desk designs with verses, my journals where I can see them, and more. This is actually how my current business of interior design with a "divine twist"; Inner Radiance Design, was born.

ALL of the above, STEP BY STEP, is still part of the journey to the inner you to later manifest a better you in all your relationships and in your life. Live the life you are intended and designed to live!

SMALL PRAYER

If by now you feel the need to accept the Lord as your Savior, it means that since you are serious about this life-changing need, you are willing to release all control to the only one who has all control, God alone. Read it nice and loud, and confess it with your mouth.

> **FATHER IN HEAVEN, HOLY IS YOUR NAME,** and **THANK YOU FOR THIS OPPORTUNITY OF ACCEPTING YOU IN MY LIFE. I ASK YOU TODAY TO COME INTO MY HEART AS I ACCEPT YOUR SON JESUS CHRIST AS MY LORD AND SAVIOR. WRITE MY NAME IN THE BOOK OF LIFE AND CLEANSE ME OF ALL MY SINS. HELP ME IN THIS WALK BY FILLING ME UP WITH YOUR ANOINTING OF YOUR HOLY SPIRIT AND THIS NEW START. IN JESUS NAME I PRAY.**
> **AMEN**

CHAPTER 9

CONTENTMENT IN ALL SEASONS

You are probably thinking easier said than done and yes you are right. I learned four key scriptures (there's more found within the promises we discussed earlier in the book but for the topic on Contentment, three were the biggest impact) that brought revelation to my life. I will share them with you, but you must truly study them, pray for them, and declare them over your life so that your spirit can internalize them. Revelations given to a person will always be hard to explain it forward, so I will try my best right now!

I memorized:

Psalms 40: 1-3

1. I waited patiently for the Lord; And He inclined to me, and heard my cry.

2. He also brought me up out of a horrible pit (Spanish version: says the PIT OF DESPERATION), Out of

the miry clay, set my feet upon a rock, *and* established my steps.

3. He has put a new song in my mouth— Praise to our God; many will see *it* and fear, and will trust in the Lord.

These verses kept my perspective focused on the fact that we focus so much in going in to the next season of our lives, or what we want, and what we don't want that we go into a desperation for our next season or moments, which truly hurt our soul (mind, will, and emotions). I began to see in these three verses, though the entire chapter is a blessing that God truly inclines to hear me because He loves me and desires to hear what I have to say. **He takes me out from all pits, even those I put myself into.** He re-establishes me, and not because I'm going somewhere or the next season, but because He places new worship on my lips. Praise (giving him thanks for the things He has done), no matter the situation. To really unravel the ugliness of the feeling of desperation, you see the anxieties behind it, the sadness, the unhealthiness, the pity, the pain, and the lack of self-love. But our Father loves us that much, unconditionally, that HE RESCUES us either way. This begins to form a heart of gratitude and contentment in all seasons. Lows or highs!

> He takes me out from all pits, even those I put myself into.

Philippians 4:11- Paul says he learned to be content. It reads: ¹¹ Not that I speak in regard to need, for I have learned in whatever state I am, to be content.

Many disregard the word content, as if it's something negative if you start claiming you are content. As if now you are NOT human and you no longer feel pain or grief or hurt. It's not what its content means. Contentment in the Greek means to be fulfilled and satisfied in life without needing anything externally to add to that inner fulfillment. Full gratification no matter the situation. Even in the midst of negative situations, you can still experience the joy of the Lord that still sustains you and loves you. But secondly many want to ignore the word LEARNED. Paul says he learned to be content, which means we can as well. You learn something by practicing it enough, repetition, intentionally, and disciplining yourself. Learning comes with action, my friend!

Psalm 23:1 was key in this learning process; The Lord IS MY SHEPHERD, I shall not want.

To want something means you have an expectation of receiving something. I remember listening to a great teaching explaining Psalm 23:1 by a pastor's wife, and she used herself as an example and said "she learned to release all expectations from her husband because she can now appreciate anything he may do." This truly impacted me! I took it to a new level in a new revelation. It's not about lowering standards in your life, it's true that the same way Jesus gave His life, without expecting back from us, and to have the hope of a relationship with us, same way we need to release all expectations from people, from any relationship, and give unto them without expecting back. Moreover, removing expectations from everyone including God because He doesn't owe me anything. I'm not worthy of His death, yet He chose to lay His life for you and me, allowing me to really have a more appreciative, grateful heart, of any small token done towards me from anyone at any given moment. Anything received, anything done for me, it all comes to me now as a bigger act of love done by any individual. Even to the point of being able to see God's Love acting through the individual, even if they were a stranger. You begin to see the only that should take all the glory for all good deeds, the loving Father!

> **"ONLY WHEN YOU GET TO THIS POINT OF CONTENTMENT IN YOUR LIFE YOU GET TO UNCOVER A NEW MYSTERY OF THE KINGDOM; CONTENTMENT IS FOUND SOLELY BECAUSE YOU REMAIN IN GOD's PRESENCE"-**

You remain in the secret place, the Holy of Holies! When this occurs your life will revolve around wanting to fulfill your calling on this Earth to obey and please the Lord, your Lord, the master, King, and owner of your life!

Then this brings you to a final revelation that propels you to go into serving the Lord wherever He calls you to... therefore you finally embrace and acknowledge that...

John 12:20-25 *"a grain of wheat must die, and fall into the ground, so that it can multiply"*

This verse brought truth to my life, where it revealed that there are times we must be stripped away of everything so that we can finally

"His way- the right way."

let God restore, and resurrect everything He wants for us **His way- the right way**. I was able to see that I had to truly feel as if I failed and lost it all so that He can remake me, and now make me whole and able to give fruits in Him!

CHAPTER 10

IT'S ALL ABOUT THE CALLING AND PURPOSE

This is when the human wants, desires, and worldly things are diminished in you; in such a way that you begin to claim and believe that truly everything that matters is fulfilling the calling even when you do not fulfill anything else in life. For example, getting married, having children, the career of your dreams, the white picket fence and the luxury vehicle. Where your first love- now being the Lord- remains in His first "rightly so Position." Whether you have or do not have, you have everything because you have Him. I came to understand that having anything else without Him being first, is not worth it. Putting God first in my life provides me the opportunity to pour, bless and love on others purely. Also, understanding that anything added on to my life, it's exactly that, just *add-ons, not goals*! The goal, the focus is: that is truly all about the calling and purpose!

> **Purpose is when you serve that thing you are most passionate about. That which fulfills you. Yet it's also when you serve forward what broke you the most in life to still give GOD the glory.**

My friend, we have gone through tough difficult situations in our lives. In which all are NOT for you to keep, they are to share forward to help another soul find inner healing, and the God of Peace, Joy, and Love.

To find the God that can restore their life that it's in pieces and make a masterpiece. To find the God that can straighten the life that it's distorted. You will begin making decisions as simple as who, what, where, and why are the things you are doing- because you want them to always and at all cost to be aligned with the calling and purpose.

Understanding the fact that I must uncover and fulfill the calling over my life allows me to be radical, bolder, and always willing to renew my mind for God alone. I finally understood that everything is of Him, through Him, and to Him for His glory (Rom 11:36). Through us all individually God wants to show His glory and as a result, all your relationships, your character, and simply you will radiate and reflect that! His glory! Always, Always, push to reflect God's original plan

that He had for women and men to live in harmony and that everything done would glorify Him.

> **It was His perfect plan and it still is!**

One impactful encounter that I had in my life that truly allows you to see that it's all about the CALLING:

I remember somewhere around the age of 24 years old, already serving in ministry, going to a sport's club just to please a friend who wanted to go there for her birthday. She knew I liked Salsa at the time so she mentioned the place plays a lot of salsa. I remember I had already sort of stopped going to clubs and anything of that nature so I did not feel comfortable with going, but still went- to PLEASE A FRIEND. When we arrived everything was ok, it was a lounge environment with big screens to watch the game while you drank and had a "good time." I never enjoyed drinking, my fun was in dancing therefore; if I wasn't dancing – meant I was bored. About 45min in I remember standing by that corner high top table we were in, and having a vivid "SLOW MOTION" (trance) vision where everything stops and in a split second I hear a voice within my Spirit that says in SPANISH **"what are you doing here when you know you don't belong here?"** And I heard it repeated a second time as my eyes and my peripheral sight did a 180-degree look in the entire room WITHIN that "split second vision." That shook me because the FEAR of the LORD consumed me and I knew- that I knew that it was GOD who spoke to me. I share this testimony to tell you that at that moment I understood "IT IS TRULY ALL ABOUT THE CALLING" God wasn't saying or concern with saying; "hey you are sinning for being in here, hey this or that it's wrong"–HE SAID **"YOU DON'T BELONG HERE"** reminding me that

> "what are you doing here when you know you don't belong here?"

HE already saw me in my destiny –THAT'S WHERE I BELONGED- it was further beyond what I can imagine or think of! And the exact same words I DECLARE and remind you of you today!

"YOU DON'T BELONG HERE"

> **You belong where HE SEES YOU! Fulfilling your calling and purpose!**

To my single ladies, wait on God, and let Him unite Him with the man that is best for you and that together you both elevate IN PURPOSE!

I pray this book has blessed your life, in the same manner that it has blessed me in serving you by writing it to help your needs. If there is something I've learned throughout this journey of this book is the fulfillment I do get when I see a woman or man be free because they are living out their intended life, no longer distorted behind the lies of the enemy! Be free, and free indeed!

Remember to go deeper in other hidden distorted designs I encourage to join me in the journey through the next book: STRIPPING AWAY THE VEST where I share direct personal encounters and experiences that GOD showed me while in the NYPD to share with women just like you and be enlighten and help transform to a Radiant Woman in deeper levels- and to help any man understand them as well!

{STAY CONNECTED RESOURCES on the last page}

YOUR INTENDED LIFE WORKBOOK

INTRODUCTION

I never realized how many relationships I was affecting, the anxieties and sporadic depression I was fighting, the cycle of toxic relationships I was confronting.

Please list 3 emotions that you're struggling with.

1. _____

2. _____

3. _____

"A CAN OF EMOTIONS THAT NEED _____"

Allow me to serve your needs by sharing the journey, secrets, and practical things to be RENEWED and get you to the Best Intended life God made for you!

Please List 5 things you need to fix.

1. _____

2. _____

3. _____

4. _____

5. _____

Be honest with yourself and let's start this journey together.

I'VE BEEN THERE TOO

Just like in simple math, the common denominator was I and is always ME in everything good or bad that it's happening or has happened in my life!

List 4 "ME" Pride issues your dealing with?

1. _____

2. _____

3. _____

4. _____

I knew I had such a need for a _____
that I did not want to go back to the old _____.

REMEMBER THIS: "YOU ARE NOT HERE ON EARTH JUST TO EXIST! There's a PLAN BEYOND your situations, sickness, circumstances, and worries."

I WAS IN DENIAL!

Thus, denial is a cognitive process that is an attempt to alter our experience of unwanted or unacceptable emotions. We can use denial to hide from any negative emotion.

It cognitive process Includes:

1. Shame

2. Fear

3. Guilt

4. Distress

Please connect these Denial triggers.

My shame is

___

___

___

___

I fear

___

DISTORTED

_____

_____

_____

I was guilty of

_____

_____

_____

I was guilty of

_____

_____

_____

"The mind has to be _____
to cause _____."

YOU MUST DETOX, WHAT YOU BELIEVED TO BE RIGHT!

I'll tell you the secret; you need to literally DETOX! Unlearn the learned things, get cleansed from what you believe is right and get rid of some of it, if not all of it.

Listed are the 3 steps I took to Detox.

1. I am "very visual", so I went back to that LIST of the **negative** and **positive** impacts and I literally prayed to God to help me be open in the areas I thought I was correct and to open my eyes to see and be enlightened when there was room for improvement.

Write down 3 positive impacts in your life.

1. _____

2. _____

3. _____

I made the decision to let it all go when it pertains to an area that I acknowledge I needed help in, understanding me, who I was, and the things I have learned.

What 3 things do you need to "Unlearn"?

DISTORTED

1. _____

2. _____

3. _____

Through my daily walk whenever I spoke to anyone, women or men, I was carefully thinking of my thought process, intentionally seeing from which root it is coming from

What is the one thought you need to Guard Most?

_____

_____

_____

_____

BE INTENTIONAL!

I WAS OPEN AND WISE ENOUGH TO MAKE THE BOLD DECISION OF UNDERSTANDING "THE SOUL"

The Devil, the enemy, wants to get to your **subconscious**, which is in our **mind,** which is in our **soul**, so that the will can decide, hence the **body** may act on it, and he does it through:

- MUSIC

- SHOWS

- MOVIES

- CONVERSATIONS, etc.

Everything is connected to your 5 senses:

- Sight

- Smell

- Sound

- Taste

- Touch

Questions to Ponder on:

- What are you watching?

- What are you feeling?

- What are you touching?

- What are your connections?

- What is your atmosphere?

And these are only to name a few of the drastic changes to consider. You must ask and answer these questions to yourself.

Key biblical life principle: "Everything is permissible in life, but not everything is beneficial."

As you can _____, understanding the _____ took me to a deeper _____ that I had no idea it would _____ me too.

BE OPEN TO STARTING A PRAYER LIFE, IN A BOLD RADICAL WAY

"To have more of God you must learn to do less for a season" Cave Time Inventory:

What are things you need to bring to the Cave? What are things you need to leave in the Cave? What are things you need to take from the Cave?

I know it might sound radical, BUT I wanted radical change.

List 3 Radical changes you have to do this year.

1. _____

2. _____

3. _____

"Contentment is tied together with enjoying your new season and in this season appreciate all that you have and do not have. I came to an internal state at heart where I did not want anything else but Christ."

DISTORTED

REVELATIONS STRAIGHT FROM ABOVE!

The Revelation of His STILLNESS.

    Stillness is trusting God.

    Stillness isn't always quiet and picturesque.

    Stillness is hearing his Voice.

    Stillness is seeing Him move in your favor

    Please jot down 4 distracting thoughts.

1. _____

2. _____

3. _____

4. _____

Listed in no specific order, these are SOME of my revelations:

He is truly my _____, no matter whatever my earthly _____ had or haven't done.

Be _____, we do not know it all, and is ok to accept that you are still l_____

Learned _____ in ALL seasons of life and NOT TO _____

KEY POINT: The REVELATIONS I would write them down. I would read my entire list day and night, until about one and a half years later when my character truly began to look a bit more like the Jesus who rescued me, and I highly recommend for you to do the same.

- YouTube Channel: MARLYN ROJAS OFFICIAL; where I personally give the last 3 chapters workbook on Video.

Also...

SERVANT, **Marlyn Rojas**, is Honored to continue serving you and the multitude by BOLDLY RESTORING IDENTITY, DESIGN, LOVE, RELATIONSHIPS, & PURPOSES through Him.

STAY CONNECTED VIA:

- DISTORTED is available on tour for Women Conferences &/or Book Clubs.

- WOMEN FACEBOOK PAGE: Radiant Woman International

- INSTAGRAM: @MarlynRojasOfficial

- TWITTER: @MarlynRojas

- FACEBOOK PAGE: @MarlynRojasOfficial

- PODCAST: MarlynRojasOfficial By Marlyn Rojas (on seven plus platforms)

- All Books available on Amazon, Barnes & Nobles, and Many book Distributors.

- SCHEDULE Your Certified Intl. Life & Relationship Coaching Session/or Radiant Publishing Consult TODAY at: www.MarlynRojas.com

Additional SERVICES Available: Radiant Publishing (coaching authors, including publishing/ministry/podcast coaching) | Ministry | Conferences | Workshops | Teachings

| Preaching | Interpreting Services/Class | Workshops | @LasRojasSisters | Inner Radiance Designs | by Grace, Ordained Minister serving at Local Church.

www.ingramcontent.com/pod-product-compliance
Lightning Source LLC
Chambersburg PA
CBHW071320080526
44587CB00018B/3292